INDUSTRIAL RAILWAY LOCOMOTIVE SHEDS

A Pictorial Selection

by
Adrian Booth

INDUSTRIAL RAILWAY SOCIETY
2012

© Adrian Booth, 2012
Reprinted April 2015

ISBN: 978 1 901556 81 0

Front cover picture: Newmarket Colliery

Published in 2012 by the
Industrial Railway Society at
26 Great Bank Road, Herringthorpe,
Rotherham, South Yorkshire, S65 3BT

www.irsociety.co.uk

Produced for the IRS by Print Rite, Freeland, Witney, Oxon. 01993 881662

Introduction

The majority of older enthusiasts will probably admit to starting their hobby as a British Railways steam 'shed-basher', and enjoying touring the country's sheds in search of numbers for subsequent underlining in a treasured *Ian Allan Locoshed* book. Shed bashing became like a drug to many enthusiasts, with every weekend spent visiting different areas. This could take the form of a string of visits made in organised parties, who hired a motor coach and usually had a set of admission permits, officially issued by BR. Other enthusiasts would go it alone, visiting sheds via directions provided by the invaluable *Ian Allan Shed Directory*. My personal local shed was Canklow (coded 41D) which I started visiting soon after my train spotting initiation as a nine years old lad at Rotherham Masborough Station. During the 1960s, with dieselisation proceeding rapidly, it became increasingly difficult to obtain written permission from BR for groups to visit sheds, and some enthusiasts used to sneak in uninvited. At Canklow this was usually by means of a path which ran to the rear entrance, where a deep breath was taken before plunging into the roundhouse with its ever-attendant danger of discovery and ejection by the shed foreman. They were great days, with sheds providing anticipation, excitement, atmosphere, and enjoyment.

BR steam came to an end that sad day in August 1968, when I went on the Dalescroft Railway Society's coach trip to witness the last rites at Rose Grove, Lostock Hall, and Carnforth. Suddenly steam had gone on British Railways and, for many enthusiasts, there was a feeling of 'what do we do now?' Fortunately I had already discovered industrial railways, where steam locomotives still reigned supreme at many sites around the country, although diesels were rapidly encroaching there too. I started visiting industrial sites in 1968 and those early days were a voyage of discovery into hitherto unheard of locomotive builders, plus the sights and sounds and smells of collieries, power stations, and sewage works.

1. North Gawber Colliery, Barnsley, on 17th April 1974 with Hunslet 3212 of 1945 viewed through the unglazed window frame.

I immediately discovered that most industrial sites had a locomotive shed and, in the spring of 1968, the first four that I looked round were Orgreave, Brookhouse, Dinnington and Firbeck collieries. These visits made such an impression on me that I can still vividly recall ex-BR 68077 at the back of Orgreave shed, and gazing upon a stately old green Avonside simmering outside Dinnington shed. Perhaps industrial sheds did not provide the quantity of locomotives, when compared to a typical BR steam shed, but it was still possible to experience the familiar atmosphere and smells of the steam age.

2. North Gawber Colliery shed on Christmas Eve 1977, with the roof removed and the inspection pit filling with water. Hunslet 3788 of 1953 stands in the background.

In the 1970s and 1980s it was quite easy to visit industrial establishments on an official basis, if you had the time and enthusiasm to organise things in advance. The modern paranoid obsession with Health and Safety regulations had not been invented and so a letter with SAE would usually receive a positive response. On-spec visits were also nearly always allowed, with staff generally delighted to have someone show an interest in their establishment. A guide would be provided and, besides looking at the locomotives, you normally obtained interesting information about the works' history, and often were shown the manufacturing processes. It was all a wonderful education. Of course, if time was of the essence, it was possible to revive the old thrills of bunking. Over the years, I made numerous unofficial visits to establishments, and successfully looked round the sheds – although on occasions I must confess to having been 'asked to leave'!

On many of my official, on-spec and 'unofficial' visits, a wide variety of locomotive sheds was encountered. It is true that the average industrial structure was certainly not a 'northlight' with numerous roads, or a roundhouse with a turntable, although there were exceptions, which was all part of the charm of industrial railways. For example Beckton Gas Works had a roundhouse, Corby Quarries a ten road shed, and Nostell Colliery a turntable, but the average industrial shed was more likely to be a one or two road dead end structure. At small sites the sheds were often lacking in decent facilities, and sometimes there were holes in the roof, with the doors either dropped or rotted off. On the other hand, some sites had modern structures with roller shutter doors and first class maintenance facilities. But all this variety gave industrial railways their character. As on BR, however, steam was gradually phased out and by the early 1980s it had almost disappeared completely. Dieselisation never dampened my enthusiasm for industrial railways, however, and my visits continued over the years, although nowadays there are but a fraction of the total number of sites of old.

There have been many books published about mainline sheds (steam and diesel), and whose photographs recapture the atmosphere of those establishments, and the happy times enjoyed by enthusiasts in visiting them. So far as I am aware, however, no volume has been published about the more humble industrial shed, and my book now seeks to put that right. Every industrial shed was totally independent and there was no BR-style system of shed-codes, so alphabetical order has been used to determine the order of the photographs. The systems depicted are standard gauge unless otherwise noted in the caption, and references to 'left' and 'right' are when looking towards the shed.

All the photographs were taken by me in the period from 1968 to the mid-1990s. The majority of the sites depicted have either closed or dispensed with internal railways, and the sheds have been demolished or turned over to other uses. Nevertheless, I hope my pictures prove to be of interest to all readers. In conclusion, I wish to thank Keith Gunner, Dave Marden and Robert Pritchard for kindly proof-reading my manuscript, and Andrew & Jane Smith for preparing my book for the printers.

Adrian Booth
Rotherham, 12th August 2012

3. Aberpergwm Colliery was located at Glyn Neath in West Glamorgan, and utilised a rare Becorit 200mm gauge 'roadrailer' surface railway. A flameproof diesel hydraulic locomotive (Becorit DRL 40/3/512 of 1973), stands on the left of this 24th April 1978 view, waiting to operate a manriding train down the 1971 drift. The corrugated iron 'Becorit Locomotive Garage' (per sign at roof apex) is on the right. Note the points arrangement in the foreground, where the hinged plate at the junction was swung across when access to the locomotive shed was required, and secured by a bolt hole through the rail being matched to a hole in the base-plate.

4. Acton Lane Power Station was at Harlesden in Greater London, and was the last location in the capital to operate steam locomotives. The shed was erected around the buffer stops situated at the end of the parallel twin running roads, and had a concrete coal stage, extreme left. It was a corrugated sheeting structure, with a pit on the right hand road, and in this 10th September 1979 view the twin doors were ajar to reveal their two steam locomotives: BIRKENHEAD (Robert Stephenson & Hawthorns 7386 of 1948) and LITTLE BARFORD (Andrew Barclay 2069 of 1939). This pair shared duties until the end of rail traffic.

5. Allerton Bywater Colliery was located just to the north of Castleford in West Yorkshire. In the 1970s and 1980s they had a fleet of diesel locomotives used for yard shunting and also taking spoil, loaded in rakes of side-tipping wagons, along a branch to tipping points beside the River Calder. The fleet was housed in this attractive shed, but note that two sections above the entrance had been roughly repaired with corrugated sheeting. The left hand shed road was capable of holding three locomotives and was provided with a full-length pit, with a dividing wall between it and the workshop facility, right, which held just one locomotive and also had a pit. This 11th June 1983 view shows number 42 (Andrew Barclay 592 of 1974) and 46 (Thomas Hill 248v of 1974) standing on the shed road, with 39 (Hunslet 7278 of 1972) peeping out of the shed. Under cover behind the Hunslet were 44 (Hunslet 6684 of 1968) and 43 (Andrew Barclay 593 of 1974). Number 47 (Thomas Hill 249v of 1974) is on the workshop road (right) whilst 45 (Yorkshire Engine Company 2674 of 1959) was just off-camera.

6. Annesley Colliery was near Kirkby in Ashfield in Nottinghamshire. When this photograph was taken on 7th March 1981 rail traffic had ceased and the 'Beware of locos' sign on the old shed wall was redundant. Track still ran into the attractive two-road slate roof shed, however, which had a green roller shutter door on the left hand road, and a wooden sliding door on the right. Although the building was provided with three windows in the right wall, there were none in the left.

7. Appleby Frodingham is a huge steelworks complex at Scunthorpe in Lincolnshire which operated over sixty diesel locomotives in the mid-1970s. As befits a fleet of this size they had a large four roads shed, with red brick lower walls, perspex windows, and a corrugated iron roof. The two outer roads had full length pits, whilst the two centre roads each had a small pit at the rear, and all four comfortably held three Yorkshire Engine Company 'Janus' diesel-electric locomotives which were the mainstay of the fleet. The two roads workshop facility (and the bike shed) was to the left, and a small wooden wagon turntable was situated between the two buildings. The photograph was taken on 5th May 1979, when 20 locomotives were on shed (including 17 Janus types), and this was probably as near as industry got to the atmosphere of a BR diesel shed.

8. Appleby Frodingham steelworks at Scunthorpe again, this time on 24th March 1978. GEC Traction 5435 and 5439 of 1977 stand on the left, whilst Janus number 13 (Yorkshire Engine Company 2715 of 1958) on the right receives attention from a fitter.

9. Ashington Colliery in Northumberland was one of the country's best-known coal mines, utilising a large fleet of steam locomotives to shunt an extensive railway network. When steam gave way to diesels the location, if anything, became better known due to their use of several ex-BR D95xx 'Paxman' locomotives. The attractive shed was of red brick construction, with sixteen side windows, eleven smoke/fumes vents, corrugated sheeting roof, and wooden doors. When viewed on 20th April 1987, the building held five 'Paxmans'.

10. Askern Colliery, together with its associated large coking plant, was located a few miles due north of Doncaster, in South Yorkshire. Its locomotive shed was an aging brick built structure with a flat roof, and had two roads, each provided with double wooden doors. On 3rd June 1971, a class 165DE 0-6-0 diesel electric (Ruston & Hornsby 384146 of 1956) was standing outside, in the company of a work worn 0-6-0 saddle tank with heavily stained chimney (Hunslet 3594 of 1950).

11. Barony Power Station was operated by the South of Scotland Electricity Board, at Auchinleck, Strathclyde, and was designed to burn slurry from local collieries. The shed was a prime example of a purely functional building, with scant regard to aesthetics at the design stage. It was brick-built, forming part of a wider garage block, with an inspection pit, grey roller shutter door, and three windows on just the right side. On 10th June 1981, Andrew Barclay 515 of 1966 was the sole occupant.

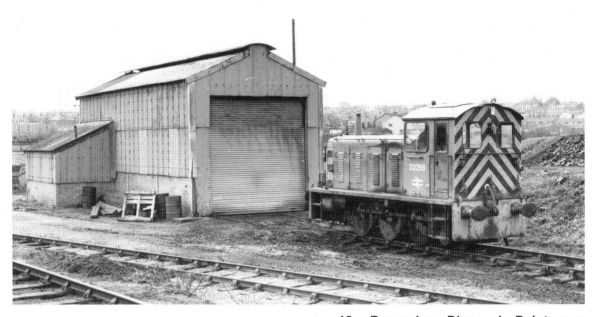

12. Bennerley Disposal Point was operated on behalf of the National Coal Board Opencast Executive by Lindley (Plant) Ltd. The shed was of brick construction to approximately five feet, then corrugated iron sheeting above, and had a grey roller shutter door. A pit was provided inside, with a little mess hut for the loco crews at back left. Ex-BR shunter D2258 was standing outside on 5th April 1983 and, although many examples of this type were sold from industry to preservation, it was not so lucky, being scrapped in 1986 at C.F. Booth Ltd's yard in Rotherham.

13. Bersham Colliery was located at Rhostyllen in Clwyd. Its shed was an ancient brick-built structure with corrugated iron roof, a long redundant light above the entrance, full length pit, and whose doors had long since fallen off – although it still comfortably held the pit's Peckett and Hawthorn Leslie 0-4-0 saddle tanks. The shed yard had, sadly, been reduced to a 'Site for refuse burning' (as per the notice, lower right) when photographed on 23rd May 1979.

14. Bethell Gwynn was a firm of ship owners at Victoria Wharf, Plymouth, located on a quayside at the end of the BR Cattedown branch. The lines terminated at a headshunt in the remains of a tunnel, which was about 35 yards long, stone lined, and had two orange-painted steel doors – and was improvised as a loco shed. When photographed on 9th September 1995 the 'shed' was disused, rail traffic having ceased, with much track lifted and the Hibberd 'Planet' diesel (3281 of 1948) having gone in November 1993 to the Plym Valley Railway.

15. Birch Coppice Colliery was at Dordon in Warwickshire and had this attractive brick-built single road shed, which held two locomotives. It had a full-length pit, four side windows, a fire hoses box beside the left hand door, a fine set of chimneys, and a pair of hinged green painted wooden doors. On 29th October 1980 Hunslet 7396 of 1974 was lurking in the shed, where it was under repair.

16. Blackburn Meadows Power Station was in the Wincobank area of Sheffield, close neighbours with the city's main sewage works and the present day Meadowhall shopping centre. The locomotive shed was in the shadow of the massive cooling towers, extreme left, which were a well-known city feature to travellers on the adjacent M1 motorway, although now demolished. The shed was brick-built, with hinged double wooden doors, a corrugated sheeting roof, and a small workshop at front left. On 25th June 1977 rail traffic had ceased and the shed was empty.

17. Blackhall Colliery was one of a string of coastal pits in County Durham whose coal seams were under the North Sea. The colliery had a 2ft gauge stockyard railway, with a pair of diesel locomotives which were used for hauling materials tubs to the shaft for transferring underground. The shed, seen on 10th May 1978, was of red brick construction, with a corrugated sheeting roof, a side window, and double doors of differing styles, whilst the wall and roof were coming apart above the extreme left of the lintel.

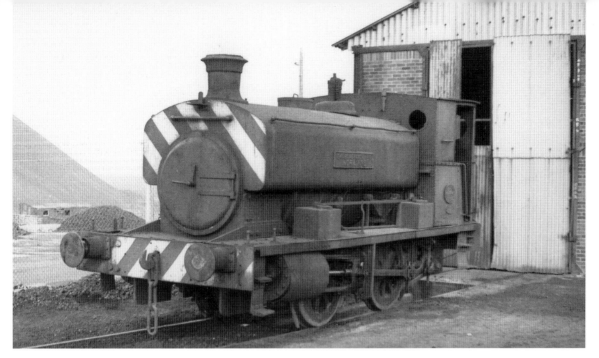

18. Blaenavon Colliery in South Wales was on the outskirts of the historic industrial town of the same name. On 25th February 1977, NORA No.5 (Andrew Barclay 1680 of 1920) was standing outside the shed, which was single road with a small mess hut in the back right corner, with a two-thirds length inspection pit inside and a smaller pit outside. It was of red brick construction, with a corrugated sheeting roof, and two yellow corrugated doors, one of which had a gaping hole.

19. Bowers Row was a coal disposal point at Astley in West Yorkshire, operated by Hargreaves (Industrial Services) Ltd on behalf of the National Coal Board Opencast Executive. The dilapidated one road shed was of corrugated sheeting construction, with gaping holes where various panels had fallen off. The facilities comprised one inspection pit and a small store at the rear. On 11th June 1983 ex-BR shunter 12099 was enjoying a rest between shunting merry-go-round wagons comprising the daily train to Immingham.

20. Bowhill Coal Preparation Plant was located at Cardenden in the county of Fife. The two-roads shed was a fairly typical old fashioned red brick-built structure with a pitched roof of corrugated sheeting. A small lean-to bothy was provided just to the right of the entrance, whose wooden door was full of holes and in danger of falling apart, whilst a sand drying furnace is on the left. The shed held four locomotives, and North British 27591 of 1957, a 440hp 0-6-0 diesel hydraulic, was resting outside on 20th May 1977.

21/22. Brookhouse Colliery was near Beighton at the east end of Sheffield, and latterly operated a couple of diesels, although Hudswell Clarke D1152 of 1959 was up on blocks (top picture) when the site was visited on 1st October 1981 and ex-BR D2229 was doing all the work. The single road dead end shed was brick built, with a row of boarded-up windows down each side, a pair of large wooden doors, a corrugated sheeting roof, a diesel tank at the front, and had a capacity of two locomotives. D1152 was at the back of the shed (bottom picture) on 12th November 1980 and the scene sums up the atmosphere of these establishments: with a bike resting against a scruffy workbench, upon which rests a set of cubby holes for nuts and bolts and various other bits and pieces.

23. Burntisland in Fife was home to the British Aluminium Company which, to the early 1970s, operated a pair of Peckett saddle tanks and a Barclay of 1937 vintage. They were housed in this shed, which was a single road, brick-built structure, with wooden double sliding doors, six windows down each side, two windows in the back wall, a full length pit, and a water tank just inside the door. On 30th September 1985, rail traffic had ceased and the tracks were overgrown. Note the old wheels in the undergrowth, extreme right.

24. Brymbo Steelworks was located in North Wales and, on 16th August 1982, AUSTIN (Yorkshire Engine Company 2855 of 1961) is seen outside the two-roads dead end shed. This was a tall, brick built structure, with steel roller shutter doors and inspection pits inside and out on both roads.

25. Brynlliw Colliery was located at Grovesend, in West Glamorgan. The single road shed was of red brick construction with corrugated sheeting above, and had a pitched roof, four windows down each side, a full length pit, and a mess hut just round the corner to the left. A narrow gauge wheelset is amongst the scrap at bottom right, whilst Peckett 2114 of 1951 can be glimpsed in the left background, on 9th June 1980.

26. Butterley Ltd had a works at Ripley, Derbyshire, adjacent to the Midland Railway Company's preservation site. On 7th June 1987 the firm still operated two diesel locomotives, of which ex-BR D2858 is seen outside the single road brick-built shed. Although at first glance an unremarkable structure, it was a candidate for the unofficial title of the UK's most secure shed. It had tight fitting double wooden doors, and all the windows were bricked up, with not the slightest chink through which the frustrated enthusiast could see the locomotives within! This was a sign of the times for, when the shed had been visited in October 1977, all windows were glazed.

27. Cadeby Colliery was located at Conisbrough in South Yorkshire, being sunk between 1889/93. The colliery had a fine brick-built shed with louvred smoke vents on the triple-pitched roof, with each of the six roads having its own wooden door. Full length pits were provided on roads three, five and six (from the left) and a dividing wall split off the two right-hand roads. The rear of the shed had a small stores/workshop, and an electricians' shop. The shed is seen on 28th May 1977 against a backdrop of the No.2 shaft, and note the bonnet cover of a Hudswell Clarke diesel, bottom right.

28/29. Cadley Hill Colliery was at Castle Gresley, to the south-east of Burton-on-Trent. It was a particularly well-known mine due to the longevity of its use of steam locomotives, and the handy adjacent public footpaths and roads for viewing. The through-shed was brick-built, with full length perspex windows, sideways moving steel 'concertina' doors, and a water crane and office at the rear. The left-hand road continued through the building, with the right having buffer stops within the shed. Hunslet 2857 of 1943, formerly of Dodworth Colliery, Barnsley, is prominent in the 25th October 1981 view (top) with EMPRESS (Bagnall 3061 of 1954) behind. Note the old wheels lying beside the shed wall. On 29th April 1977 (bottom) Hunslet 3851 of 1962 simmers at the rear.

30. Carlisle Power Station was situated at Willow Holme, alongside the West Coast Main Line, and just south of BR Kingmoor Depot. Regular steam working continued into the late 1970's, with a Hudswell Clarke saddle tank, and these two Andrew Barclay 0-6-0 fireless locomotives (2153 of 1943 and 2193 of 1944). The pair was on-shed on 16th August 1970, the doors to the brick-built two-road dead end shed having been opened for the benefit of the photographer.

31. Carrington Power Station was built on the banks of the Manchester Ship Canal, opposite Irlam Steel Works, in the western outskirts of Manchester. The two-roads, brick-built, flat roof, dead end shed had an enormous fuel tank outside, and on 10th October 1977 held, left to right, John Fowler 4210059 of 1951, rare Robert Stephenson & Hawthorns 7746 of 1954, and Hunslet 6973 of 1969.

32. Channel Tunnel was constructed by Transmanche-Link whose main site was at Shakespeare Cliff, near Dover. The massive undertaking required dozens of brand new 900mm gauge locomotives for taking men and materials into the bore, and bringing out the spoil. Security was extremely tight and there was a blanket ban on all visits. Nevertheless it was possible to view the site from the cliff top, from where a telephoto lens view of the four roads 'Locomotive Workshop' on 8th March 1992, revealed several locomotives in the immediate area.

33. Clay Cross Foundry was located to the south of Chesterfield in Derbyshire. The shed was a small single road brick-built structure, with sloping roof, whose right hand door was falling apart when photographed on 10th June 1978. The sign reads 'Danger. Beware of loco & wagons', but sadly it was no longer relevant as rail traffic had recently ceased and the two Rustons in the shed (327970 of 1954 visible) were for sale.

34. Coed Bach was a coal disposal point near Kidwelly in South Wales, and well known for its use of two ex-BR class 07 shunters. The site is seen on 2nd April 1991, viewed from the cab of 07012, with the shed prominent. It formed the end of a larger building, and was of breeze block construction with rows of windows along either side, and had a full length pit on the single track which ended at a buffer stop.

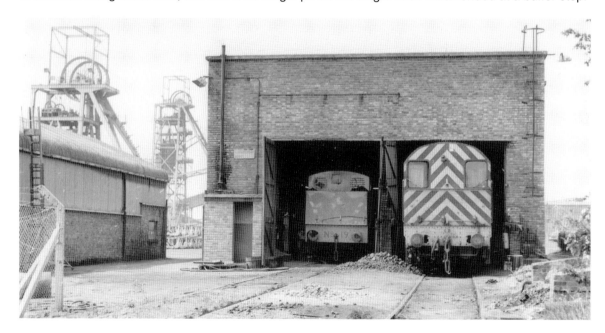

35. Comrie Colliery was at Saline in Fife. The two-roads, brick-built, flat roof shed was photographed on 31st May 1978, the colliery management having helpfully placed a sign 'Locomotive shed' on the left wall. Double wooden doors were provided on each road, although they were propped permanently open and the extreme right one had fallen off altogether. No.19 (Hunslet 3818 of 1954) is on the left, having just returned from overhaul at the NCB's Cowdenbeath Works, whilst 08425 was on hire from BR.

36/37. Corby Quarries were operated by the British Steel Corporation, with a network of branch lines bringing ironstone from surrounding quarries to the main works. They utilised a fleet of ex-BR Paxman locomotives, which were housed in an impressive eight road shed at Gretton Brook, one of the biggest industrial sheds in the UK, and provided with first class maintenance facilities. On 17th May 1980 there were 25 locomotives on-shed when D9537 (left) headed an Industrial Railway Society tour marking the end of operations on the quarry railways, with participants sitting on bales of straw in open wagons. The second picture shows a pair of 'Paxmans' inside the shed on 8th November 1975, with 61 (D9529) on the left.

38. Cornforth Quarry in County Durham, was operated by Cornforth Limestone Co Ltd, but later taken over by Tarmac. The last train left the site on 19th July 1978 and the two Ruston & Hornsby class 88DS locomotives were stored in the shed. This was a single road structure, of brick to five feet then corrugated sheeting above. The double wooden doors had been swung open on 27th June 1979 to reveal Ruston 262996 of 1949 inside.

39. Costain Concrete was situated at Newmains in Strathclyde. The company made use of its own product to construct its unusual locomotive shed, which was formed of ten precast 3ft 3in concrete sections, meeting at the apex, with steel doors and a small pit. On 12th June 1981 Ruston & Hornsby 326065 of 1952 was spare on the short spur at the rear of the shed, with the building being reserved for the working Hunslet.

40. Courtaulds Ltd operated a works at Great Coates, near Grimsby, which is seen on 24th March 1978. The single road, dead end shed was of red brick base and front, with perspex side windows and a flat roof. Hibberd 3817 of 1956 is visible inside, whilst Sentinel 9596 of 1955 (right) was disused in the yard.

41. Cowley Hill was a glass works at St Helens, Merseyside, operated by Pilkington Bros Ltd, who used a fleet of five Yorkshire Engine Company diesel shunters. On 1st December 1983 QUEENBOROUGH (2782 of 1960) was outside the three-roads, brick-built structure, which had a single pitched roof of corrugated sheeting, full length pit on the right-hand road, double wooden doors on each road, perspex roof windows, and a mess room on the right.

42. Denby Iron Company once operated a works at Ripley in Derbyshire. Their former shed (which once housed Hunslet and Yorkshire Engine Company locomotives) miraculously survived long after the company closed down and was photographed on 4th July 1976, although it was later demolished when the area was opencasted.

43. Dinnington Colliery was located near Rotherham and, on 30th May 1968, green livery 0-6-0 saddle tank BILL (Avonside 1920 of 1924) was snoozing outside the shed. This locomotive (and DAISY at the associated Firbeck Colliery) were named after the manager and his wife at the time of delivery. The shed was of one road, and of red brick construction with tall wooden doors.

44. Dowlow Works in Derbyshire was operated by Steetley Ltd when visited on 1st June 1982. The fleet comprised three Ruston & Hornsby locomotives, of which HEATHCOTE (461959 of 1961) is seen in the somewhat dilapidated single road shed of wooden construction.

45. Eclipse Peat Works was situated at Meare, near Glastonbury on the Somerset Levels. The works was operated by Fisons, and utilised a 2ft 0in gauge railway to bring peat off the moor to an unloading gantry. They had five Lister locomotives, which were accommodated in this round top, single road shed with two wooden doors and a fuel tank outside, which is seen on 22nd September 1978. Fisons was ahead of its time, with a 'No smoking' sign at the shed entrance!

46. Ely Rail Freight Terminal was operated by G.G. Papworth Ltd at the former Ely sugar beet factory, where sidings branched off BR adjacent to Ely North Junction signal box. Thomas Hill 150c of 1965 is seen in this picture dated 13th October 1986, whilst the corrugated sheeting shed only had the left hand road still insitu.

47. Empire Paper Mills was situated at Greenhithe in Kent and operated by Reeds. The small two roads shed was crammed in between a two-storey building and a brick tower, with its tracks laid in hard standing, and had an inspection pit on both roads. It was open ended with no doors, although a tarpaulin could be drawn across the right hand road. A redundant steam pipe on the right once charged the Orenstein & Koppel fireless locomotive, and chocks on the rails told the driver when he was in the correct position to commence charging. On 12th September 1979, BATMAN (Ruston & Hornsby 512842 of 1965) was receiving repairs to its engine.

48. Far Ings Tileries was operated by William Blyth Ltd on the south bank of the River Humber, and utilised a 2ft gauge railway between clay pits and the works' processing plant. On 6th May 1990, the ugly but functional Motor Rail locomotive (8678 of 1941) was standing outside the shed. This was brick built, with wooden doors and a sloping roof, and was highly unusual, in that the main running line passed straight through the building.

49. Ferrybridge Power Station was located near Knottingley in West Yorkshire. The single road shed was of red brick, with high perspex windows, an inspection pit, and smoke vent. Andrew Barclay 2360 of 1954 was resident on 16th October 1975, although disused since 1972. The shed was on the bank of the Aire & Calder Navigation, and provided the unusual sight of a row of lifebelts hanging on the inside wall.

50/51. Firbeck Colliery was situated a couple of miles to the north east of the previously featured Dinnington Colliery. The tall and elegant brick built shed is seen on 13th December 1986 (above) and had six bricked up side windows, a pitched roof of corrugated sheeting, and double steel doors. On 30th May 1968 (left) it had created an oft-found frustration, when the close confines of the typically narrow industrial shed precluded a full picture of 0-6-0 saddle tank DAISY (Avonside 1895 of 1923). She was steamed once a year for a boiler test, but had been replaced by a Hudswell Clarke diesel.

52. Fishburn Coking Plant in County Durham opened in 1954 and closed in 1986. The two roads, dead end shed was in two sections: the original left part was brick built, and had a pitched roof of corrugated sheeting, plus a steel roller-shutter door; the later right part was corrugated sheeting and had a pit at the rear. The shed was disused when seen on 30th August 1986 with Hunslet 5305 of 1959 stored on the left road.

53. Frances Colliery was located on the cliff tops above the Firth of Forth near Dysart in Fife. The single road shed had a base of red bricks, above which was a steel framework mounted with corrugated sheeting on the sides and roof. An incongruous tiny window was provided in the right wall. On 20th May 1977, the colliery was still using steam locomotives, as witness the Andrew Barclay (left) and the smoke stain above the shed entrance.

54. Gedling Colliery in Nottinghamshire was visited on 4th October 1980. Two diesel locomotives were in the shed, which was brick built, with glazed windows down each side, a pitched corrugated iron roof, and was of one road with a full length inspection pit. The two locomotives outside were SUSAN (Thomas Hill 176v of 1966) and GILLIAN (Thomas Hill 182v of 1967).

55. Glasshoughton Colliery was located on the outskirts of Castleford, and its locomotives were accommodated in a two-roads brick built shed which had an arched open entrance on the left road, but a square entry with wooden doors on the right. Hudswell Clarke 1870 of 1953 stands outside on 21st June 1969, with Hudswell Clarke diesel D1072 of 1958 within.

56. Glendon East was just to the north of Kettering and was part of the BSC's ironstone mining empire. On 3rd August 1979, the shed was in two sections with a dividing wall. It was brick built with double wooden doors on each road and a twin pitched roof fitted with corrugated sheeting. The left road held one locomotive and had a small office building at the rear, whilst the right road held two locomotives and had four side windows. Both roads had full length pits.

57. Gresford Colliery was situated near Wrexham in North Wales. On 26th July 1970 the roster was four steam locomotives, all by different builders, of which THE WELSHMAN (Manning Wardle 1207 of 1890) was standing in the shed yard. The plain and functional single road, dead end, flat roof, brick-built shed contained RICHBORO (Hudswell Clarke 1243 of 1917) standing just inside.

58. Guinness Brewery is noted for its legendary dark stout but, on 10th September 1979, had other attractions at its Park Royal site in London. The company's pair of Hibberd diesels were housed in this one road dead end shed, constructed of corrugated sheeting with two steel doors, and having two small inspection pits and five side windows.

59. Gwaun cae Gurwen was an opencast site in South Wales, operated by Powell Duffryn. On 17th August 1994, ex-BR shunter 08113 was undergoing repairs at the back of the shed. This was a two roads structure, with the right road being longer than the left and provided with an inspection pit. The shed was constructed of a base of five layers of breeze blocks, with an inner steel framework supporting middle rows of perspex windows, and a top section and roof of corrugated sheeting. There was an overhead crane with a safe working load of two tons.

60. Hams Hall Power Station was in Warwickshire, where the CEGB generated electricity for the City of Birmingham. On 22nd April 1978, 0-6-0 side tank No.9 (Robert Stephenson & Hawthorns 7151 of 1944) was standing alongside the shed, a two roads structure of red brick construction, with flat roof and steel roller shutter doors on both roads.

61. Hartlepool Steel Works was in County Durham, on the north east coast. On 10th May 1978, it had a fleet of some two dozen locomotives and, to service them, utilised this large, secure, unattractive, flat roofed, functional shed. It had two roads, with roller shutter doors, and a large fuel tank outside. Standing in the shed yard was number 455, a rebuild of Sentinel 10041 of 1960 undertaken by Thomas Hill Ltd to its own works number 259c of 1975.

62. Hindlow Works was located a couple of miles to the south east of Buxton, and operated by ICI when visited on 1st June 1982. Hibberd 'Planet' 3892 of 1958 was standing outside the shed, which was brick built, with two roads, each of which held one locomotive and was provided with an inspection pit. The facility was completed by a lean-to (right) and a secure store (left).

63. Holmes Works at Rotherham was operated by J.J. Habershon & Sons Ltd. Viewed on 23rd March 1979, this red brick building was originally a shed used for a locomotive out-stationed by the Parkgate Iron & Steel Company, and later used by Habershon's to house their own Sentinel steam lorry (to 1938) and thereafter their Kent Construction petrol locomotive. It was known as 'the dolly shed'.

64. Kilvington Gypsum Works was in Nottinghamshire and operated by Associated Portland Cement Manufacturers. Mineral was transported from quarry to works on a 3ft 0in gauge railway and, on 2nd May 1979, Ruston & Hornsby 281290 of 1949 (100DL class) was standing outside the single road shed, which was constructed of corrugated sheeting, and had double doors, plus a half length inspection pit at the front end.

65. Knostrop Sewage Works was operated by the Yorkshire Water Authority on the outskirts of Leeds, and featured one of the most interesting narrow gauge (1ft 11½in) railways in England. On 13th July 1979, Motor Rail works numbers 1369 and 1377 of 1918 (ex-WD 40hp armour-plated locomotives) were outside the shed. This was a beautifully built, stylish, solid brick building with six arch-shaped glazed windows down each side, twin chimneys, and an arched entrance with roller shutter steel door. A broad inspection pit ran the length of the building, with track resting on a central brick support and lengthways girders.

66. Ladysmith Washery was situated at Kells, to the south of Whitehaven. It was served by a dramatic railway which ran along the cliff tops, linking the washery to Haig Colliery and an incline to Whitehaven harbour. On 9th July 1974 Andrew Barclay 1974 of 1930 was simmering in the entrance to the near derelict single road shed whose doors had fallen off and which had gaping holes in its roof.

67. Lagoon Sewage Works was located at Water Orton in the West Midlands and operated by the Severn Trent Water Authority. It was served by a 2ft 0in gauge railway, with a fleet of Motor Rail locomotives which were housed and serviced in this four roads, flat roof shed at nearby Minworth. It contained ten locomotives when viewed on 26th April 1978.

68. Langwith Colliery was in north Derbyshire and its last coal was wound in June 1979. On 28th August 1979, redundant Hudswell Clarke D1279 of 1963 is just visible inside the one road, red brick shed with corrugated sheeting roof. The brickwork reveals the shed originally had an arched entrance.

69. Laxey shed on the Isle of Man was owned by the Civil Aviation Authority. On 17th June 1986, the shed was brick built, with windows down each side, double wooden doors, a rear side door, and corrugated sheeting roof. A single 3ft 6in gauge track ran into the shed, which housed two railcars by D. Wickham of Ware, works numbers 7642 of 1958 and 10956 of 1976 which were painted in black and yellow livery.

70/71. Long Marston in Warwickshire was the HQ of the MoD Army Engineers, and had an extensive railway system. The MoD utilised a modern running/servicing shed, plus this separate round-top storage shed (top) of corrugated sheeting, with red brick ends and corrugated sheeting doors. On 26th September 1984 (bottom) the shed held 150hp ARMY 229 (Drewry 2183 of 1945) and ARMY 221 (Bicester of 1955).

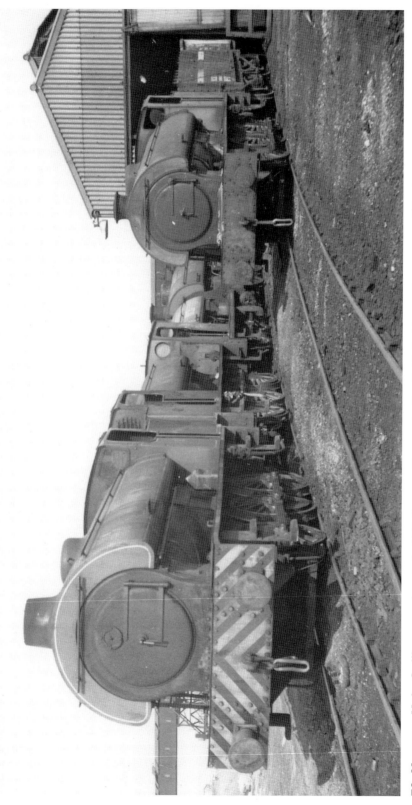

72. Manvers Main Colliery was located at Wath upon Dearne in South Yorkshire and was one of the biggest coal complexes in the country. The two roads shed had a base section of red brick, upon which was erected a steel framework with corrugated sheeting, and there were smoke vents in the roof. On 7th June 1969 there was a busy atmosphere with no less than sixteen locomotives on-shed, of which Hunslet 3889 of 1964, Hunslet 3685 of 1948, Yorkshire Engine Company 1823 of 1922, Peckett 1891 of 1940, and Hunslet 3834 of 1955 are visible.

73. Mardy Colliery was the anglicised name of the pit situated at Maerdy, near Ferndale in the Rhondda Valley. On 13th May 1975 ex-BR shunter 12054 was standing outside the extremely rudimentary, brick built, flat roofed, single road shed. Note the three pairs of wheels laid beside the left hand wall.

74. Markham Main Colliery was located at Armthorpe, and was the last Doncaster area colliery to use a steam locomotive. On 16th October 1975, Hunslet 3782 of 1953 was in steam outside the shed, which was brick built with a corrugated sheeting roof, roller shutter doors, and could accommodate two locomotives on each of its two roads, both of which had an inspection pit.

75. Marshall Fowler had a works at Sprotbrough, near Doncaster, and latterly utilised a unique prototype diesel, John Fowler 4120001 of 1951. It was housed in this somewhat basic, single road, dead end, red brick shed, viewed on 17th March 1978.

76. Measham Colliery was situated just to the south west of Ashby-de-la-Zouch in Leicestershire, and closed in the aftermath of the 1984/85 miners' strike. Viewed on 25th September 1985, the disused shed was of brick construction, with full length perspex windows, and corrugated sheeting upper walls and roof. The entrance had steel concertina doors and (per writing above) gave 14ft 6in headroom.

77. Mexborough Sewage Works in South Yorkshire was opened about 1968 and utilised a mono-rail system to serve the 32 sludge drying beds. On 25th November 1980, their Metalair Ltd built machine (a combined driver's cab, 7bhp Hatz engine, and skip, located on one frame) is seen reversing into the brick built shed, with flat concrete roof, side windows, and up-and-over door. The section of rail beneath the door was lifted out and stored in the shed, to enable the door to be closed.

78. Midhurst Whites manufactured white bricks at its works at Midhurst in Sussex. The works utilised a 2ft 6in gauge rail system for bringing sand from the pits and tipping waste into a disused pit. On 11th September 1979, two Motor Rail locomotives were present, of which 6035 of 1937 was standing outside the single road shed (in sylvan setting) which had a corrugated sheeting roof and double wooden doors.

79. Middlewich Salt Works in Cheshire was run by the British Salt Company. On 22nd July 1983, the single road, dead end shed was brick built, with a pitched roof of corrugated sheeting, a single chimney, three glazed windows on each side, steel roller-shutter door, and a full length inspection pit. One of the residents was ex-BR shunter D2150.

80. Midland Yorkshire Tar Distillers had a couple of works in Yorkshire, and the Kilnhurst site was visited on 9th August 1977. The single road, brick built shed, had the track off centre, providing an area on the left for the accommodation of stores and equipment and workbenches for the loco fitters.

81. Mode Wheel, at Weaste, was the operational headquarters of the Manchester Ship Canal Company's railway section which, at its zenith, operated the largest industrial railway system in the UK. Six tracks serviced the workshops and paint shop, and two central sidings separated it from the three roads running shed. By 13th August 1983, the MSC railway was but a shadow of former glories and rows of disused Hudswell Clarke diesels occupied the roofless shed, whose roads were known as the 'cemetery road' (right, named after the facility over the wall), the 'middle road', and the 'sandhole road' (left, as it ran alongside the sand drying furnaces).

82. Mostyn Docks are on the North Wales coast, just to the east of Prestatyn. On 23rd May 1979, Yorkshire Engine Company 2819 of 1960 was residing in the shed, constructed of breeze blocks, with pitched roof of corrugated sheeting, three small windows on each side, and a full length pit on the left road only.

83/84. Mountain Ash in South Wales served Deep Duffryn Colliery, Penrikyber Colliery and Aberaman Phurnacite Plant. The shed, on the banks of the River Cynon, and seen on 23rd April 1979, was a dilapidated structure, with signs of clumsy rebuilding, featuring stone and two types of red brick (right) plus white and red brick (left) indicating that the roof was raised at one time. Internal inspection pits, broken concrete floor, filthy walls, arched windows, hosepipe, rows of strip lighting, workmen's lockers, and a corrugated sheeting roof with many gaping holes, completed the spartan facilities. The second picture shows Hudswell Clarke 1885 of 1955 and ex-GWR/BR 7754 standing outside on 8th November 1974.

85. Mountain Ash had thirteen locomotives on site on 24th April 1978. Resting in the shed (left to right) were: Peckett 1859 of 1932, Andrew Barclay 2074 of 1939, Avonside 1680 of 1914, and ex-GWR/BR pannier tank 7754.

86. Mountsorrel Granite Quarry was operated by Redland Roadstone and, on 26th April 1975, Peckett 1759 of 1928 was inside the shed, beneath some substantial wooden smoke vents. Its right side was covered in stone, which had burst in through the caved-in shed wall, but it was subsequently dug out and went for preservation to Market Overton in June 1978.

87. Nechells Power Station was located in Birmingham, and operated by the Central Electricity Generating Board. It was an all steam stronghold until the early 1970s, but when visited on 26th April 1978 diesels had infiltrated. Ruston & Hornsby 275886 of 1949 was standing outside the corrugated iron shed, seen across the Birmingham & Warwick Junction Canal. A tiny flat trolley stands up against the shed door.

88. Newdigate Colliery was located at Bedworth in Warwickshire. The two roads, dead end shed, seen on 25th April 1979, was brick built, with a corrugated sheeting roof, five windows down each side, double steel doors on each road, a pit on the left road, and a fuel tank at the rear.

89. Newmarket Colliery was at Stanley in West Yorkshire and the two roads shed was photographed on 11th June 1983. The original shed (right) was of red brick construction and had a corrugated sheeting pitched roof, but the second road (with a flat roof) was added later and the dividing wall taken out. A large diesel tank was on the flat roof, whilst an inspection pit was on the right road which held Thomas Hill 154c of 1965. Sentinel 10182 of 1964 is on the left.

90. Newstead Sewage Works was at Blurton, Stoke on Trent and operated by the Severn Trent Water Authority. On 31st July 1978, two Motor Rails were operational on the works' 2ft 0in gauge system, and housed in this pleasing brick built shed. The works closed in 1986.

91. New Stubbin Colliery was at Rawmarsh, Rotherham, and closed in July 1978. On the 24th of that month several large cracks (due to subsidence) were evident in the brickwork of the two roads shed, which had double wooden doors on each road and a 5 tons crane outside.

92. Normanby Park steelworks was situated in Scunthorpe, Lincolnshire. The complex did not have a conventional locomotive shed, but utilised a modern CEW – Central Engineering Workshops – where various types of equipment were repaired. 'Steelman' number 56 (Rolls-Royce 10277 of 1968, left) and five Sentinels are in this view dated 24th March 1978.

93. North Devon Clay employed a small and quaint railway, which would not be contemplated today. On 21st September 1978, Fowler 4000001 of 1945 had shunted the day's four loaded wagons, whilst another Fowler (22928 of 1940) resided in this little single road shed in a sylvan setting.

94/95. North Gawber Colliery was on the outskirts of Barnsley, and provided a rare example of an industrial through shed. On 28th June 1969 (top) Andrew Barclay 2195 of 1945 was standing outside the single road shed, of red brick construction, with corrugated sheeting roof, partially glazed side windows, a row of smoke vents, and an inspection pit. It provided an atmospheric sight (bottom) on Christmas Eve 1977, with old wagons and a veteran steam crane standing disused on the left, whilst an Austerity (Hunslet 3788 of 1953) is just visible on the right. The dilapidated shed had seen better days, with the roof now removed and the glass missing from all the windows.

96. North Sea Camp was located at Freiston, near Boston, and operated as an open prison for lower category offenders. An extensive 2ft 0in gauge system was utilised by prisoners to assist with works on sea defences, and also around the farm where crops were grown for prison service canteens. On 1st June 1990, five Lister locomotives were on site, one inside this shed of breeze block construction with curved corrugated sheeting roof.

97. Nostell Colliery in West Yorkshire had two sheds when visited on 30th September 1981. One shed (long disused) was unremarkable in itself, but was one of the great rarities of UK industrial railways, as it featured access via a turntable. Of wooden construction, the turntable was contained within a brick lined pit, from which radiated six roads: the approach road, two shed roads, and three open locomotive stabling roads. Hibberd 3865 of 1957 is seen standing on the turntable.

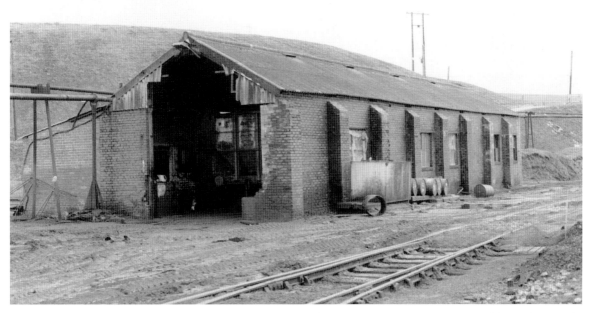

98. Onllwyn Disposal Point in South Wales utilised this shed, viewed on 11th April 1985, which could comfortably accommodate their trio of English Electric 0-6-0 diesels. It was a single road, brick built structure, with five side windows, a full length inspection pit, and a corrugated sheeting pitched roof.

99. Orgreave Coking Plant, near Rotherham, had a small fleet of Yorkshire Engine Company diesels, of which 2528 of 1953 is seen on the left of this view dated 1st January 1980. The fleet was maintained in this tall, brick built, spacious, warm, elegantly designed and well equipped shed/workshops.

100. Orgreave Colliery shed is seen on 20th March 1977, and was a brick built, single road facility, with twelve side windows, corrugated sheeting roof, and double wooden doors with a notice 'SLOW 5MPH' to their right. The site (infamous during the 1984/85 coal mining dispute) is now buried following a massive open-casting and landfill project.

101. Padiham Power Station was at Burnley and, on 11th March 1978, Andrew Barclay 473 of 1961 stands alongside 'No.1 Fuel Tank' outside the two roads, flat roof, dead end shed. This was of corrugated sheeting construction with steel concertina doors.

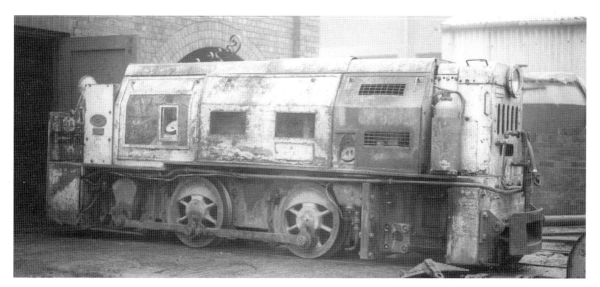

102. Park Mill Colliery was located at Clayton West, near Huddersfield. Drifts were driven about 1950/51 and 2ft 6in gauge flameproof diesel locomotives used from 1951. Working locomotives remained underground, with the shed (at the top of the inclined materials drift) used only for repairs and servicing. On 12th January 1980, DEBORAH (Hudswell Clarke DM1356 of 1965) stands outside the shed, with the arched drift entrance behind.

103. Penmaenmawr Quarry (operated by Kingston Minerals) had this lovely shed at a 3ft 0in/standard gauge/conveyor interchange located between the BR main line and the ship loading jetty. It was of concrete construction, with two wooden doors, vertical wooden boards above the doors, one side window, a slate roof, brick chimney, wooden smoke vent, and had an inspection pit. On 23rd May 1979, the shed held Ruston & Hornsby 202987 of 1941, although inside was a relic from when the building accommodated a DeWinton steam locomotive – a handle in the roof which, when wound, dropped the shed chimney down to fit snugly over the locomotive chimney.

104. Philadelphia in County Durham was home to the two roads running shed of the National Coal Board's famous Lambton Railway. Photographed on 26th June 1979, it was a classic example of how, in the 'old days', companies did not skimp during construction, as witness the elegant row of fifteen inset arched windows, all complete with stone sills.

105. Plymstock Works was at Plymouth in Devon and operated by Blue Circle, who utilised Thomas Hill 125v of 1963 for shunting cement tanks. On 18th September 1978, the 28 tons locomotive is seen standing outside its stylish single road shed.

106/107. Polkemmet Colliery was at Whitburn in West Lothian, and provided visiting enthusiasts with the spectacle of steam locomotives working hard up a long gradient, taking loaded coal wagons to the exchange sidings. On 19th May 1977 (top) Andrew Barclay locos 1296 of 1912 and 1175 of 1909 were standing beside the water tank outside the somewhat functional two roads shed. On 17th August 1977 (bottom), Andrew Barclay locos 1296 and 2358 of 1954 were outside, viewed past dismantled parts of Barclay 885 of 1900, with 1175 inside the shed undergoing repairs.

108/109. Pontardulais shed yard in South Wales (top) on 24th April 1978. The single road shed was of red brick construction with corrugated sheeting roof and double doors, and could accommodate two locomotives. An awning on the left provided rudimentary cover for one locomotive standing outside, although even this was lessened by several holes in its dilapidated roof. The track on the right ran over a level crossing behind the shed, before continuing up to Graig Merthyr Colliery. On 9th June 1980 (bottom) Bagnall 2758 of 1944 was beneath the awning and 08818, on hire from BR, stabled between duties.

110. Port Penrhyn near Bangor in North Wales is fondly remembered as the terminus of a six miles narrow gauge railway which once transported slate from Penrhyn quarries. Operations had long ceased on 24th May 1979, although the elegant two roads shed survived, built of stone, with brick lined arches, and (of course) a slate roof.

111. Preston Docks in Lancashire had a modern and well equipped shed, constructed of corrugated panels mounted upon a brick base, and in stark contrast to Penrhyn (above). Viewed on 1st September 1983, Rolls-Royce 10283 of 1968 was standing inside.

112. Pye Hill Colliery was located in Nottinghamshire and, on 7th October 1977, Ruston & Hornsby 395293 of 1956 was standing in the shed yard. It was unofficially named I'LL TRY, the catch phrase of its cantankerous regular driver! The functional two roads shed was of red brick construction and provided with heavy sliding wooden doors.

113. Queenborough Rolling Mills was located on the Isle of Sheppey in Kent and featured a lengthy branch down to a rail-served pier. On 7th March 1992, six locomotives were on site, of which number 15 (Bicester of 1955) was standing outside the shed. This was a two roads structure, built entirely of corrugated sheeting.

114. Raisby Quarry was near Coxhoe in County Durham and reached by the single track branch (left). The single road shed was constructed of brick, and provided with a pit and double wooden doors. On 26th July 1982, Sentinel 10077 of 1961 was locked inside.

115. Renishaw Park Colliery was located just to the north of Staveley, and connected to the Rotherham to Chesterfield 'Old Road' railway. On 31st May 1982, the small, single road, brick-built, flat roof shed, had No.13 (Hudswell Clarke D1279 of 1963) standing at its entrance.

116. Rhoose Cement Works in South Wales was operated by the grandly named Aberthaw & Bristol Channel Portland Cement Co Ltd. On 12th June 1980, PRIMROSE (John Fowler 4210121 of 1956) was inside the brick built shed with roller shutter doors. This could hold two locomotives on each road, with a full length inspection pit on the left road and an outside pit on the right road.

117. Rowntree Mackintosh operated an extensive internal railway at their famous chocolate factory at York. On 20th June 1979, Ruston & Hornsby 423661 of 1958 was shunting alongside the two roads dead end shed, constructed of red brick, with side windows and a pitched roof laid with corrugated sheeting. Inside the building was a 5 tons overhead crane.

118. Salwick Works at Preston was operated by British Nuclear Fuels Limited, but rail traffic had ceased on 9th October 1993. The solidly constructed red brick shed had roller shutter doors, although it had been reduced to only one road, upon which the newly preserved Hudswell Clarke D628 of 1943 was standing.

119. Saville Colliery was at Methley in West Yorkshire. By 11th June 1983, rail traffic had ceased and Hunslet 7260 of 1971 was disused outside the single road brick built shed, complete with inspection pit, corrugated sheeting roof, and bricked-up side windows. Hudswell Clarke D1070 of 1958 was stored at the front of the shed.

120/121. Seaham was a fascinating industrial town in County Durham. Seaham Colliery (top) was one of three pits in the town and, on 3rd August 1983, Andrew Barclay 523 of 1967 was outside the single road, brick built shed, with double wooden doors. The Harbour Dock Company (bottom) operated a railway along the cliff tops. In 1967 SHDC replaced an aging steam fleet with five new 305hp English Electric diesels and, on 14th April 1989, D4 (EEV D1194 of 1967) was inside the brick built shed, which had a sloping roof.

122. Shap Granite Company was located alongside, and connected to, the famous West Coast Main Line incline. On 28th September 1984 the company's only locomotive, Sentinel 10186 of 1964, was resting in the one road dead end shed, of red brick construction, with pitched roof laid with corrugated sheeting.

123. Shelton Steel Works was operated by the British Steel Corporation. On 31st July 1978, the two roads shed was constructed of corrugated sheeting, with double wooden doors on each road, and a tall diesel tank outside. The left road ended at an internal buffer stop although the right road emerged for a short distance at the rear.

124. Shilbottle Colliery in Northumberland had a well built two road shed, with a brick base, upper half of substantial corrugated sheeting, and an impressive smoke/fumes extraction system on its roof. On 21st May 1977, ex-BR diesel D4068 peers out at the redundant water crane, with a notice 'No smoking – diesel oil' on the front left wall.

125. Smithywood Coking Plant was at Chapeltown, near Sheffield, and was one of the very last locations in the UK to use steam locomotives. On 1st June 1980, Hunslet 3888 of 1964 was in steam outside the single road shed, of red brick construction with corrugated sheeting roof.

126. Snowdown Colliery was one of the small number of pits in the Kent coalfield, and noted for its Avonside steam locomotives, although ex-BR diesel 15224 is prominent on this view of 13th September 1979. The attractive shed was of red brick construction, with two red roller shutter doors, and had a full length pit on both roads, three windows and a door on the left side, and four windows on the right side, whilst the pitched roof had a smoke extractor and four chimneys. A water tank and water crane were provided at the front.

127. South Kirkby Colliery was near Barnsley, and employed three steam locomotives when visited on 28th July 1972. KINSLEY (Hunslet 1954 of 1939) was standing outside the single road shed, which was of red brick construction with front upper panelling beneath a single pitched roof.

128. Steel Peech & Tozer (later BSC) was a large steel maker with works situated at Ickles and Templeborough, in Rotherham. On 13th May 1979 the small, corrugated sheeting, single road shed was overflowing, with Yorkshire Engine Company diesels 2, 31, 25 and 23 standing outside.

129. Stourport Power Station in Worcestershire probably had the UK's most unusual locomotive shed. Seen on 26th September 1983, this single road, brick-built structure, with five side windows, was at the very end of the rail system, amazingly perched atop a reinforced concrete lattice gantry.

130. Sunderland Docks' two roads shed was constructed around 1982 of inner breeze blocks lined with bricks, and topped by a single pitch roof lined with corrugated sheeting. It had roller shutter doors and three side air vents. On 14th April 1989, Ruston & Hornsby 165DE class locomotives (395294 of 1956 and 416210 of 1959) are seen outside.

131. Sutton Colliery was at Sutton in Ashfield in Nottinghamshire. On 10th July 1982 the substantial shed (of brick base with corrugated sheeting above) housed Thomas Hill 191v of 1968, whilst Sentinel 10073 of 1961 was standing in the yard.

132. Swinden Limeworks was in North Yorkshire. On 1st April 1983, their locomotive fleet was housed in this rudimentary three roads shed of breeze blocks base with a steel framework supporting sides and roof of corrugated sheeting. Ex-BR 15231 and 12083 are prominent, with Hibberd 3893 of 1958 on the right road beneath what appears to be an internal loading gauge!

133. Teesside Steelworks had a large fleet of diesel locomotives that, on 10th May 1978, over-flowed around this four-roads shed. It had a brick base, with an interior steel framework upon which was mounted walls and roof of corrugated sheeting, and numbers 251, 100, 266, 259 and 243 are outside. This site was later abandoned, and replaced by a new shed/workshops adjacent to the A1085.

134. Thakeham Tiles in Sussex operated a 2ft 0in gauge railway to bring sand from nearby pits which was used in making various tiles and blocks. On 11th September 1979, a blue Hunslet was locked in this small shed, constructed of breeze blocks, with double wooden doors and a single pitched roof mounted with corrugated sheeting.

135. Thurcroft Colliery, near Rotherham, had a highly attractive single road shed, which was built of brick, with four arched side windows, brick chimney, double wooden doors, corrugated sheeting roof and full length fume extractor. On 8th March 1978, ex-BR shunter D2334 was up on blocks outside.

136. Tower Colliery at Hirwaun in South Wales sent its coal via a conveyor (left) to a separate railhead, where its locomotive shed was located. This voluminous two roads dead end building had a brick base and internal steel framework, upon which was mounted a series of corrugated panels. Ex-BR D3261 was resting between duties on 8th June 1980.

137. Treeton Colliery was near Rotherham. On 7th March 1978, Yorkshire Engine Company 2913 of 1965 was standing outside the single road shed. This was brick built, with a roof of corrugated sheeting surmounted by fume extractors. The view shows the style of arched, multi-pane glazed windows (prevalent in the South Yorkshire coalfield) which were a throwback to the days of steam.

138. Vane Tempest Colliery was situated on the cliff top at Seaham in County Durham, and had a single road brick built shed, with five arched side windows, corrugated sheeting roof, circular front window, wooden double doors and six smoke extractor vents on the roof. No.41 (Ruston & Hornsby 421438 of 1958) was outside on 3rd August 1983.

139. Warner & Co in Middlesbrough was a firm of iron refiners that produced high quality pig iron for foundry purposes using a twin cupola unit. On 15th June 1979, their solitary locomotive (Ruston & Hornsby 417894 of 1959) was poking out of the shed. This was a single road dead end edifice, constructed of red bricks, with a corrugated sheeting roof, arched doorway, and a side bothy.

140. Waterside was located at Patna, near Dalmellington in Ayrshire, and was one of the UK's finest latter-day steam locations. At 7am on 2nd July 1973, Andrew Barclay 2284 of 1949 was preparing for work (complete with supplementary wagon 'tender') outside the shed. This was of four roads, with brick base, corrugated sheeting roof, sliding doors, full length smoke vent at the apex, and access door in the left wall.

141. Whatley Quarry in Somerset is nowadays known as a large railhead with class 59 locomotives hauling heavy stone trains. On 22nd September 1978, things were more low-key, as three small Thomas Hill diesels grouped outside ARC Southern's single road shed.

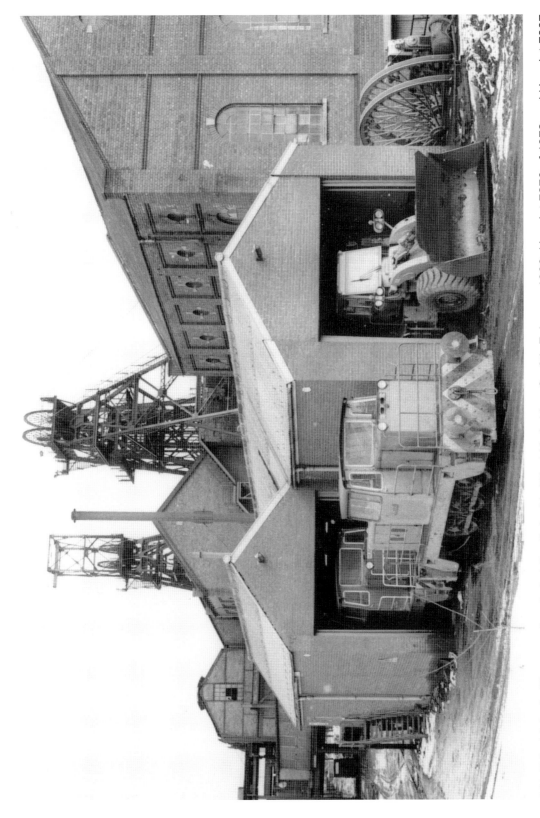

142. Wheldale Colliery was located at Castleford in West Yorkshire. On 8th February 1986, Hunslet 7276 of 1972 and Hunslet 7307 of 1973 are seen in this view of the two part dead end shed, of which each section was brick built with a corrugated sheeting pitched roof. A usurper occupies the right road!

143. Widdrington NCBOE coal distribution point was in Northumberland. On 8th November 1987, the single road, dead end shed, was of brick construction, with corrugated sheeting roof and double doors.

144. William Colliery was located close to the harbour at Whitehaven. The two road dead end shed was a crumbling edifice on 9th July 1974, although it still provided a home for Hudswell Clarke 1814 of 1948 which was illuminated by sunlight streaming in through holes in the roof. The shed was of stone construction with a roof of wooden beams supporting corrugated panels. The left road held two locomotives and had a full length inspection pit, while the right road stopped half way into the shed.

145. Wirksworth Quarry in Derbyshire was operated by Tarmac. On 5th August 1978, the locomotives were housed in a single road dead end shed which – appropriately – was constructed of stone, and had a corrugated sheeting roof with fumes extractor vent, bricked-up side windows, and double wooden doors, and was provided with an inspection pit.

146. Workington Docks in Cumbria on 22nd July 1980. The shed was brick built with timber panelling above the entrance, and had two full length inspection pits inside, plus further pits outside, but had no doors. Thomas Smith steam crane 19063 of 1951 stands outside, whilst 211 (Yorkshire Engine Company 2628 of 1956 – left) and 213 (John Fowler 4220012 of 1961 – right) are inside.